THE ZOO

PITT POETRY SERIES

Ed Ochester, Editor

THE ZOO

JOANIE MACKOWSKI

University of Pittsburgh Press

Published by the University of Pittsburgh Press, Pittsburgh, Pa., 15260
Manufactured in the United States of America
Printed on acid-free paper

10 9 8 7 6 5 4 3 2 1

This book is the winner of the 2000 Associated Writing Programs' Award
in Poetry. Associated Writing Programs, a national organization serving
over 150 colleges and universities, has its headquarters at George Mason
University, Tallwood House, Mail Stop 1E3, Fairfax, Va. 22030.

Acknowledgments are located at the end of this book.

ISBN 0-8229-5768-x

*The publication of this book
is supported by a grant from
the Pennsylvania Council
on the Arts.*

FOR MY FAMILY

CONTENTS

THE ZOO

ANTS

Two wandering across the porcelain
Siberia, one alone on the windowsill,

four across the ceiling's senseless field
of pale yellow, one negotiating folds

in a towel: tiny, bronze-colored, antennae
"strongly elbowed," crawling over *Antony*

and Cleopatra, face down, unsurprised,
one dead in the mountainous bar of soap.

Sub-family Formicinae (a single
segment behind the thorax), the sickle

moons of their abdomens, one trapped in bubbles
(I soak in the tub); with no clear purpose

they come in by the baseboard, do not bite,
crush bloodless beneath a finger. Peterson's

calls them "social creatures," yet what grim
society: identical pilgrims,

seed-like, brittle, pausing on the path
only three seconds to touch another's

face, some hoisting the papery carcasses
of their dead in their jaws, which open and close

like the clasp of a necklace. "Mating occurs
in flight"—what better way? Weightless, reckless

rapture: the winged queen and her mate, quantum
passion spiraling beneath the tamarisk,

and then the queen sheds her wings, adjusts
the pearl-like larvae in their cribs of sand:

more anvil-headed, creeping attentions
to follow cracks in the tile, the lip of the tub,

and one starting across the mirror now, doubled.

THE CLEANING

Violated, imagine, a world so mild,
where orange angels drift

sideways, zebras ascend, and predators
are not allowed. Yet I saw hands

reach in. Of course, you'll find partisan schools,
factions, minuscule

tooth marks in a chiffon veil—and small
tetras striped like Italian

flags advancing toward the blackchin mouthbrooder,
who is massive, neon,

and dimpled. The medium is liquid,
the hierarchy rigid:

Jack Dempsey is ugly and feared, the kissers
kiss only themselves,

cardinals glide upward, and some fish do not
move at all. They hang

like paisley on wallpaper,
deeply conscious of being

waiting-room decorations. A bleeding heart lurks
outside the little green pagoda. And the fish

seem out of touch, even
drugged, until

one darts
from behind the pagoda toward the crumb that mingles

with substitute sky, and staring an instant
beyond the crumb, perhaps it feels the ripples and notes

the peculiar differences between its world
and ours. The air

in the psychiatrist's waiting room
does not agree with the fish.

They sense in it
a preoccupation with interiors,

and the fish have worked millennia
for their brilliant exteriors. Some person waiting

may try to lock eyes with one, say,
with the empathetic blushing angelfish,

but the angel's flat face
disappears, into a line, like the image on an old television

screen. Was it a violation? Not one fish was removed,
but their world condensed to a desperate

level. A man in green coveralls siphoned
out water, scooped

out the terra-cotta gravel and rinsed it
in a pail. Each plastic foxtail, fern, hornwort,

and some that looked like shaving brushes
he uprooted and cleaned, and then

his yellow hand, in a rubber glove,
sponged the insides of the tank

while the fish were pressed beneath the surface.
And then from buckets, for minutes, new water

poured in; the tank's lip rose back
to the black rim. A slow,

dream-paced avalanche of gravel convulsed
a bubbling effervescence to rival

the iridescence of the fishes' scales. And again the hand
contemplatively probed, rerooted plastics,

returned the green pagoda
to its corner, and withdrew.

Bellow-
ing skull heavy with brains
of pale prunes,
the eyeballs' continual dual eclipses,
cochlear snails coiled below
the skin, ellipses

of moles
trailing off mid-sentence
and the dense
shelf fungus of lungs. Crooked teeth. The nipples'
beribboned tambourines, miles
of intestines, ripples

of jagged
coastline where a gull glides
from the clouds
and over the fingers' ten shallow, brackish bays.
Pupas, polyps, checkered
crimsons, the steady buzz

of that
locust the heart. Liver
flies over
the stomach caw-cawing, over cells buttoned down
for evening: and hear the *thud*
thud as the pudenda

fall open
to the lines: "The world is
wholly his
who can see through its pretension." But then what's left
to have? Stranded upon
the rocks as the rocks drift

off, both
too overwrought and too
naked, who
crouches here, hiding behind her shadow (turn a-
round, *look*—), dead in the path
of the navel's tornado?

THE BEAM

You love when the oak leaves shimmer like silver,
and you love the Emergency Man.
You hear him running, the blood in your veins
in the cold dawn.

He's on the highway, then at your doorway,
now his face in the frame of your window,
hand on light switch, foot on stair,
foot on shadow.

A medical tickle, he's come to repair
your *no no no*, the base
blot in your brain, your ganglion briar,
your stumbling pulse

abuzz with dirty frequencies,
your kisses, wrinkles,
and bloody
gills.

Ailing, alien, alone,
are you ill in your ear or in error?
He presses his stethoscope to your hand,
pulls a pill from the air,

he tastes your tears, taps the burl of your breast,
and he feels the cool curls of your bones.
His fingers press through your skin
where the ground opens.

And every moment's *emergency*,
all your atoms singing his name,
what a wonderful crisis, crickets sing in the grasses,
the clock goes numb—

the stinking weed he uproots from your lungs,
the snail from your skull, aphids
he plucks from your liver, your thick blue-black,
your little fits

of minor thunder—he takes you away
and leaves you limp,
your head full of light,
the beam of his lamp.

Lightning reaches down like turkey feet
toward the dozen cottages by the beach,
and a pale peach

shadow fades behind the dumbstruck corn.
A station wagon hurtles down the road,
hits every rut—

the road is like the surface of the moon.
Go that way, and the road will take you further
than you'd rather

if you ever reach the end of it;
go this way, and the road dives in the sea,
and folks in the cozy

cottages watch the moon dive in as well,
sometimes. The evening seems drawn in pencil.
The air is salty,

and diesel fumes mingle in it, or gin,
and far off the cough of another engine
comes slow—imagine,

an indifferent angel drops a pin
from the clouds, and it will fall forever—
and the countryside hovers

above itself now in the afterglow
of the flash; another, and the corn's
long as gunshot—

this coastline's delicate enough to hold
in the palm of your hand, which you stretch out
beneath the flash-lit

evening, level with your eyes: the road
grows from your fingers, two barn swallows veer
up through the V

by your thumb, the ocean feels like cornsilk
on the back of your hand, then lightning jabs
your finger—so you drop

your arm as a woman in a floral
dress pedals by you on a bicycle.
Rain soon! she calls

and weaves toward the beach, toward home? Or maybe
just to watch the glowing breakers tumble
on the shore you held

until she came. And why not hold her too?
Why not let her roll across your thumb
so she may fathom

your human fingers stretched across the sea?
Surely she'd ride as softly on their tips
as these raindrops.

WAITING

The cafe walls are covered with pictures of flying parrots;
I take a table, rest my arms; the table gently tips.
A dozen strangers sit and talk, all they do is lovely,
and tea leaves circle in their cups like hawks above the valley.

A woman reads a magazine, flicks ashes on the table;
a man pushes his plate away while fifty angels pull.
Outside a light snow's coming down, and it heaps the cars with pillows;
the waitress hums a tune off key and stacks a plate with apples.

I'm waiting on this cloudy evening, in fumes of cake and diesel,
so I find a book. It's not mine; it must be somebody's. "O-
klahoma is part of the great plains, rich with swaying grasses;
every winter is cold as death, and every summer blazes."

I find that book predictable, so I go to find another,
but the shelf is nearly empty now—only one book there:
a pictorial history of bullfighting, written by Señor Pendu;
it's always nice to be reminded that knowledge is abundant.

The spine is stained with coffee, the pages in shreds and tatters;
but it's chock full of glossy photos of famous matadors.
On page seventeen, five hungry bulls wait tied beneath a tree;
I read, "The arena's full of blood, sand, grace, and poetry."

I thumb through pages absently while waiting for a fellow.
A man approaches my table; he pauses, then says, "hello."
I'm not quite sure if he's the fellow I agreed to meet—
does our memory make us strong, or does it make us timid?

The sky outside is charcoal gray, the clouds in shapes like carrots;
the air in here is charcoal gray because of the cigarettes.
All the glowing cigarette butts are wee lighthouses in a row.
Cars outside flick their headlights on to know the world they narrow.

While waiting for God's fingertips at last to touch Adam's,
I count the ridges on the forehead of each sad Madame.
There're fourteen thousand seven hundred and a dozen ridges;
where the land is flat as milk the sky bends down and drinks.

The teacups knock about like bones, the chairs like summer thunder;
A woman puts her fork down; she smells of lavender.
Out in the street a car doesn't stop, so it bends another's fender.
The woman runs out through the door screaming, "Our brains are starving!"

While waiting, I've forgotten why, in this Cafe Paradiso,
I practice an arcane meditation, and I feel my body dissolve.
The sugar is not so enlightened, and floats in my tea like diamonds—
it must demand its nothingness, demand to lose its dazzle.

A gentleman on a bicycle pedals before the windows;
let's all turn into seagulls now and go wherever the wind goes.
Let's all be free as milkweed, free as the eye's wonders,
and inside every sugar bowl's an Oklahoma winter.

Let's all be as free as atoms, as free as Armageddon,
as free as all of god's angels who can't count up to ten.
Let's all crawl into burlap bags and play with roadside kittens;
let's live by the airport and stuff our ears with cotton.

While waiting for my rendezvous, I order a turkey sandwich
and finally hear the thread-like voice coming from my wrist watch.
"Tut tut," it says, "your eight-ball's sunk. Life's moving on without you,"
oh well, I say, so long, farewell, *auf Wiedersehen, adieu*—

But still waiting for their destinies in a stupid cafe
twenty tea drinkers get down on their knees, and they begin to pray.
It's good to pray while the tea steeps, whenever there's time to kill;
the waitress prances like a horse, laughs, "life is such a tickle."

While waiting agitatedly in the paradise I made, o-
le, ole! the vases say, and they throw their roses down.
So I draw my little sword, I kill the stumbling bull,
and blood, sand, grace, and matadors fall onto my pillow.

Slowly, at the far end of a room,
a woman is drowning. She tries to catch
the attentions of some others in the room,
who drink coffee or cocktails; some watch her
out the corner of an eye, some stare
out the window. One who watches is pleased
to note that her drowning evokes a lake
rimmed with swaying cattails, lily pads
dappling the surface. He forgets the room,
and paisleys on the sofa start to bloom;
beside the sofa, the lamp's a snowy egret
on one leg. Yet another sees a rugged, craggy
coast with a twisted Monterey cypress,
and a woman tucked into the elephant-ear
fold of a wave. The woman seems to take
some pleasure in drowning, whole moments
choking, throngs of life in the merest drop
of artificial water examined beneath
an imaginary microscope: *O bare*
paramecium of luxurious despair,
dancing on the wrong end of the pin.
Yet another sees no lake, no ocean:
he holds his glass to his eye and watches
her thrash in his vodka sour, considering
how her struggle is like a dance, as heat
and cold both sear the fingertips, extremes
uniting in the convoluted mean,
if beauty weren't so goddamned hard to bear.
Surfacing an instant, the woman lifts
her drink, smiles, her skin a resilient blue.

Clustered on the bay, fifty pelicans
rise, fly circles, dive—each angular
as origami, newspaper-colored—
and demonstrate the lazy elegance

of predation. A thick curtain of fog
just now lifts partway, lending the narrow
bay a look of surprise, a limbo
look between certainty and doubt, as, fig-

shaped, bright orange, a bumper broken
free of the dock drifts toward Point Reyes,
across the ripples compounded of grays
and gray-blues, gray-greens. Two tiny, bracken-

covered islands sit just beneath the band
of fog. One seems to be sinking; the other
is larger, dotted with gulls. And the farther
ground of the point, in rolling patches of sand

and green, slowly grows clearer. It's high tide.
Waves lap the pier. More pelicans spiral
into the fog, grow vague, embedded in pearl,
and then down again into exactitude:

all quiet and contained. One could forget
about the ocean, kept *at bay*, or almost
forget (or almost kept). The aluminum masts
of a moored sailboat wave about like insect

antennae. At a picnic table, among
sunbursts of birdlime, read "Abbey + Derek,
Lana + Bill" carved into the wood; a turkey
buzzard glides into the branches to mingle

with the shadows of a Monterey cypress
ten feet away, and wild geranium
grows in between some barnacled, cranium-
shaped rocks. The point, the bay . . . does it suppress

or defend, that wing of land, keeping wilder
currents from this placider water?
Would this quiet pocket prefer to turn
inside out, the waves to pull me under?

LULLABY

Trumpet vine, heliotrope,

        trouble, your footsteps

soft as the moon's

        whose mumbly *amo,*

amat—no matter.

        A mole in the mulberry,

and I reckon raccoons

        in the wrinkled leaves

of night-blooming jasmine.

        Choose, what do you choose?

To be hidden in Eden

        and undone, the diamondback,

pale-bellied fang

        half forgotten, some newfangled

evil unveiled

        on the verge? So,

you are an arrow,

        a hero, an hour or

two from tomorrow,

        two million miles

of midnight unfurling

        from your fingertips, and

what do you want?

    A dime-sized winter

to put in your pocket

    or dissolve in your blood?

An ocean ashine

    with starlight and waiting

in the bottom drawer

    of the bureau to buoy you

away? A cloud or

    two? A cloudy glass

of moonlight, warmed

    and white as milk?

In a book as ample

    as a bed, you'll fold

your body between pages

    and think of footprints

crossing snow,

    the sun or a pill slipped below

your tongue; in that tangle

    of tentativeness,

slumber prowls

    just inches from your elbow.

THE ZOO

Fully clothed and delighted between bars
we watch it bare

its teeth, pacing in cages, naked in furs
(ah, a peacock's tail unfurls

a wall of eyes!), and we, too, brave the wild—but beware:
this wilderness may overpower us

just with the strength it wields to be so self-contained.
A small crowd taken

in, four giraffes traverse an arid lot.
Their bodies undulate

as if underwater, their heads float on the sky like lotuses—
while nearby, motionless,

zebras breathe in the breeze, their stripes
ever so slightly rippling.

It's high noon, and overcast, besides,
but scarlet ibises

set a flock of bright orange suns; they perch
in a freestanding screened porch,

and five toddlers, linked together with a rope,
are told not to poke

their vegetable fingers through the chain-link
fence, for behind it lounges

a tiger, whose eyebrows reverberate
as her blasé tongue browses

the velvet envelopes between her new-moon
claws. A dingy emu

now cradles in her womb three bright green eggs,
(or so the placard says),

while antelopes leap over opales-
cent sun rays; impalas

wade in pools, and diamond patterns, bird-scratches,
mark the backs of my chapped

hands. . . . At the zoo, essence and ornament
meet. Is it mental

effort that keeps the well-intentioned soul
uncorrupted by this raw

nature, this ostentatious camouflage?
Or does the leisurely

daydream, half forgot, that weaves gracefully
through the overblown grass

at the base of our brains really protect
us more? There, brown ducks

escape a widening ring, and the slate-gray
water of a grassy

pool suddenly congeals into a terrible,
dripping Gibraltar:

the hippo shows his eyes and leather armor
and sinks again. Amour?—

lunatic spasms of a kookaburra
buckle in the air;

the bird itself I cannot see; its idi-
osyncratic, giddy

call hovers generally beneath the outspread
wings of the chestnut

eagle, regal (though tied by the ankle
to a wooden anchor),

who splays his jagged feathers like the petals
of a rose. Bedazzled,

I amble through the zoo lazily
as the dazed animals.

An appendix on my memory swells, and my
pace slows, muscles

contract—prepare to spring (what ambergris
now grows in me?): some animals are angry,

I think, to be kept in cages,
but which is stronger,

the ingenuity of chain-link,
(look!) or fascination?

LIST

Remember the Alamo, remember Armageddon,
remember the mustard and chard in your garden.
Remember how alien you felt most of the day,
remember the sofa, *fa so lah ti doh.*

Remember that insects most naturally kneel,
your fluttering half-conscious acts of denial,
the water that rises, the cradle that falls,
the itinerant border between true and false.

And don't forget "impulse," or "opals," or "empty,"
to look at your hand before upping the ante,
the unopened letter that lies on the table,
the things that you wanted to say, but weren't able.

Remember the baby, its parents, the weather,
the unbounded world and the puzzling other,
the cause of a war, the caws of some crows,
that the sky stretches up, and the clouds move across.

ZEROS, VEERS,

one iridescent glimpse,
unsteady on my stalk and one hand clumsily

untying a snarl of twine—the vanishing point comes
to get me, swerves from a clump of camellias

and tiger lilies: green-crowned, ruby-throated
hummingbird. How odd to be threatened

by such imperious diminutiveness, its wings translucent,
orders of sky and foliage unloosening

from either side of it, the guttural
buzz of its flight throbbing my ear. I'm on a ladder,

its feeder in one hand, the other feeling for the eye
among papery handfuls of wasp nest barely

within reach, syrup (one part sugar to four
parts water), running down my arm. *Fear*

not, for thou art blessed among—must
have been something like this, almost

knocked to the ground by grace itself, the edge
of grace, its beak within an inch

of grazing my hand outstretched, groping—
what ungainly dread creeps in

under such wings, under the eaves
and swooped at by love's

razor glinting in the sunlight?

VIEW FROM THE BLUFF

This view's too big to see. Far below,
the scrap of beach looks like a pillow,

the breakers an uneven white fringe
on a blue bedspread, topped with an orange

bell buoy, and also see a schooner
there, gliding from the outer seas to inner,

its sail set on the ripples like a tooth.
And all rimmed by the Cascades, made smooth

by distance: watching the ducks fly Vs,
the shifting hackles of the waves,

and feeling one's idiosyncrasies dissolve,
those inconvenient edges growing soft

as that band of cirrus stretching over
the San Juans. And a great blue heron

unfolds from beneath a briar, awkwardness
part of its gracefulness; it flaps away

and dwindles to a dot against the mountains,
becomes the period to close the sentence

of its own complex-compound loveliness.
Wouldn't it be nice to fly off into the distance,

to shed the body's tinsel and disappear
while a speedboat pulls open a long wake like a zipper

on the water, and then the waves zip it up
again? To blend, each ear an eddy,

each thought some floating clumps
of kelp, and the eyes a million glances

of sunlight refracting irregular argyle
patterns across the waves, while a gull

catches a fish: to be immense and minuscule. The breakers
roll themselves up between my fingers

like cigarettes, knock swirls of agitation
from swirls of calm, while the mountains jut

from the horizon like torn newspaper, their jagged
peaks crumpled against the sound as if someone could

set it aflame, kindle its deep blue cool
and white-tipped lizard skin, checkered

with light and seaweed. Peace is oceanic,
vulnerable, oddly giddy, and not

easily distinguished from chaos, but seven islands crouch in a terrible
green secret, arranged over the water

like rocks on a picnic table to anchor the tablecloth,
to keep it from blowing away and toppling

the paper platefuls and cans of beer
(as the earth and its irregular perfections

are pressed in the swirling palms of our hands,
the means absentmindedly fondled by the ends);

all kinds of truths are anchored by these islands.

THE ORACLE

Listen to the nightingales—and listen to the door,
and if you can't be God today, then be an *objet d'art.*
The beach is white as hominy, the sea is black as tar,
and every lover plays a tune on everyone's guitar.

When love arrives in envelopes, time sets it free with knives,
but don't worry darling: no postage is enough.
Each pot of gold's a dandelion, each bright knight a knave.
Here comes the tired question—when? The answer's never never.

The rain comes down, the dog goes out, the onions burn again;
I'd love to burn for you, my dear, so why don't you be gone?
Shall I buy a wee black cat, or shall I buy a gun?
Remember what the choo-choo said? Oh yes, I think I can.

Shall we hop a paper plane and fly to Cameroon?
Shall we build a monument—or maybe we should run.
I think I'll wear a spinning globe; why don't you wear maroon?
I like a graceful gentleman. Sometimes he comes around.

An atom is a tiny egg, and all life is the nest,
and atoms on their own won't hatch; they only hatch almost.
I do not wish to speak today; Professor says, "You must."
Science is the search for truth, but that don't mean it's honest.

I think doubt is the subject here, and every tongue the verb—
and everything I've ever said's a tulip or a fib.
The oracle says, "One hot potato!" and I to her, "Oh, fab-
ulous! You louse! You lush! You lust! I lust! I lust! I lust!"

THE PRINCESS AND THE SKY FISH

The fly buzzed, abysmal, bold,
and wooed the Princess of Growingold
when the sky rumbled.

The fly rolled its massive
eyeballs at her, crept through the halls of her castle and into
her ear. Church bells

rang. But the princess fled and locked her door
against the fly, eyes black as tar, lips
soft as butter.

So the fly slipped in through the keyhole, crawled
on her nipples, her bowl of cherries, loved
the small brown mole

on her shoulder, and still the princess eschewed
the fly. She sat rigid as a hatchet
and chewed a fingernail,

wondering if she should try to flee or just tumble
out the window to bleed in a bramble—
when the sky rumbled,

clouds roared: who came speeding to slay the scab-eyed
forward fly that dared creep on her lips
and lobes all day,

that dared rub his bristles along her cheek,
touch the loop of his tongue to the nape of her neck—?
O the great crackle-crack

as the angry Sky Fish sprung from a cloudscape, gills
clenched, its shimmering leap aimed
fly-ward, gold mouth agape.

LITTLE SONG

Poor deep-dug mole, little
daisy nose, dull dun
tunneler, hunted
interior error: blue-
black plum, thumbnail-
stone brain wrapped in sunset-
colored plush, apish
earthbound blunderer,
little limiter muttering
about her skull's peri-
meter, afraid of the telephone's
nil-knell, afraid
to be crushed by the stack
of mail. Little monk
of monkey rituals,
misplaced cosmos, mustard
flowers, the wrong wrestled
angel in a rut of dumb *dum
te deum*, it's time to come
away from here—

Eye to eye with Mount Rainier, we bank
a curve and five smaller mountains grow
from behind it, trailing a decrescendo
line like teats on a dog's belly. We gape

and yawn and keep our seats for turbulence,
trying to forget we're out above
our heads, leery of the pictograph's acro-
batic exit. Back home, when we taxied out,

one bald eagle spiraled high above
the runway, skillfully within the lattice
of flight patterns: does it love a jet?—
or worship them all, or mock them, rigid

freaks that never linger, their wings
don't even flutter—Oh, we're bald and glinting
now, flush against the gooseneck sun,
raking our drooping crucifix of shade

across unsuspecting pastures. This vantage
turns the earth to pure geometry!
Tangled vegetation, in the dreamer's
distant eyes, rarefies; swooping a rage

of rigid form, we've lost our touch, our bodies
cool aluminum, our heads in the clouds,
eardrums chock with glue high in the loud,
unnatural effort of all this. . . . Time,

still beating, cranes back for the dials it left
behind, but wristwatches, oblivious,
careen ahead; they'll strap to anything—
two hours and I'll strap onto you, love.

WHAT A BIRD SAID

Flying behind my shoulders, cormorants
head for the sea, an erratic, endless
stream of them: their rain-bent, pterodactylian
silhouettes set low over mercury
waves seem a bit severe—*listen, lessons*
in love aren't always tactile: a tarot
of overturned clam shells brims in the tangled
waves; the waves are full of tattered weeds
like asterisks—maybe tonight the stars
will take a risk and bloom like barnacles
underwater—*I miss you*—red-winged
blackbirds cling to the cattails, seem to say
miss you o me too or sometimes *ole!*
and sometimes this song continues all day—

VIEW FROM THE PORCH

Tall and solitary, the gnarled fulcrum
the meadow and the marsh seem to uncoil

from, stands a wavy-limbed and cerebrum-shaped
oak; yearly it yields a little memory

to an autumn gale. The pond, a mirror
full of herring, lies behind it. Rumor

says cows drown in the pond; they credulously
sink into its gritty sand while egrets

wade in, white as fluorescent lights,
eating minnows. Oh, cicadas sing—listen

to that narcotic crescendo, that buzz
that anchors passing fancies in bizarre,

dumbstruck origins; our rigid eardrums
ripple like that brackish pond as tremors

spread from its reeds into ours. Further
east, where cirri scatter feathers

across an impassive sky, triangle-
shaped red cedars stand like soldiers, and gulls

fly over them like new moons, veering uphill
clutching oysters underneath a pillow-

pink cloud and—bombs away! sharp tesserae
now fleck the wooden, roofless porch. Eraser-

topped cattails rub dull days away and bend
beneath the accidental forms of red-

winged blackbirds—nature's artistry depends
on luxury, no? Just watch the meadow's pendulous

columbine, lupine, each loud bee's
zealous wooing of a black-eyed Susan's billowed

center like one enormous breast fringed
in yellow petals, and flocks of goldfinches

spill over like the sun. Lime-green lichen
wants to know; it cups the skinny oaks like

ears, but cool, gentle breezes agitate
the leaves with unpredictable teachings.

Here, herons stand still as andirons
by the shallow, artificial
lagoon that recoils and endures
the prolific condominiums
and golf courses which—what? Oh, a fish
jumped—which sprawl beside it. Many ho-hums

and breathing cabernets will drift
across these constrained banks today,
while golf balls, here and there, like dandruff,
fleck the eel grass. The architecture
tumbles even now ("ditto,
ditto," screams a jittery

waterfowl), two-day wonders, pre-fab—
fed up, the lagoon percolates
a tumult of mildew through new fabrics
and walls. But, why, why do our dreams
disintegrate? Ask Copernicus
there, splashing his concentric rings.

Yellow locust leaves drifting into her hair,
her orange soda, yellow jackets hovering
by our plates, drifting off. Jackhammer
somewhere—*I keep looking for the tiny*
TV camera in my head, a circular saw,
a warbler, *or maybe just a little hole*
out my skull that leads to somebody else's—
time to go. A woman head to toe
in yellow on a bicycle, yellow
"danger do not cross, construction zone"
looped around lampposts, tree trunks, ribbons
of afternoon light: the color of unreason,
as in *Crime and Punishment,* devouring
orient, invasion of the suns,
Reason in man, said Thomas Aquinas,
is like God in the world. Two hundred feet
up, dime-sized sclera-white hard hat blooms
into the black of a window, withdraws.
Clocks all 15 minutes fast: errors, roses,
iceland poppies, cyclamen, low blue flame
ceanothus, trumpet vine, lavender
blooming from a concrete crypt, needing
no excuse. Acorn woodpecker, white rump,
patch of flame on crown, orderly
ecstasy in the almost-empty
parking lot, a twenty-foot RV,
awning out, and man, yawning, stepping
from the door, index hooked through the zero
on top his can of beer, abandoned backhoe,

dust rising from the gravel beneath the wheels
of a turquoise Miata. Cracker crumbs,
wad of plastic on the hood of my car,
somebody's crackers, *There is a crack in every*
thing God has made, and sun just over
the dashboard, eye to eye with crouching star,
can't see what but glare, oh dusty windshield.
Right at light, behind gray Saturn, merge
with traffic. Sunset, lights on, off. Lights on,
Detroiters need that old time off
and on religion, it's good enough
for them, will do for them when the world's
on fire. Home. Lamp. Set out a tin of arsenic
dioxide for the ants, eat a banana,
toss peel, make bed: *It is not fitting*
that God should forgive something disordered
within His kingdom. Out again, chard seedlings,
girdling with gray rings of snail bait
under the half ring of a quarter moon,
mailbox, postcard, *Greeting from The Great Wall,*
another errant orbit, incoherence
on the prowl. Next door, dogs barking—

FALLING BACKWARD

High noon: the sun's abstract eye
slides over the awestruck

sky, clouds here and
there like bones. A heron

pierces the choppy water
with its beak—whatever

it finds is beautiful
(and fish below see a snow-white devil).

It flaps across the ship canal,
and the mundane alchemy

that drew us from the mud aeons
ago, chameleon-

green and eager for ends, reddens
my shoulders. Good riddance

to you, destiny, ta-ta ta-
boo, you small potato,

there's a shadow where I once stood.
And that shadow, on Wednesday,

yearns back for Tuesday—
what in us begs it to stay?

This morning the milk went sour, floated like clouds
in the carton. So I poured them down the drain.
Gently as that, my man's wandering.

I opened the paper, and every headline read,
"You will be sad forever."
I lay in a big bed so empty it hovered.

And out the window, the sun shone dull gray,
but just because the glass was dirty.
I tried to open the window, tried utterly.

Then I went outside to rake some leaves.
So red and gold, they swirled the ground
in the fire of creation, as I turned around.

WALKING

Evening. Walk by the zoo where orangutans
hang in the fir trees like enormous peaches,
by someone's corner plot of peas, cabbages,
and plaster fauns—do you know where you're heading?

No. As telephones ring from random windows
doused with orange in evening's execution,
mount a little hill and face the sunset gushing
a creamsicle-colored band of dizzy

sky above the rough lines of the Olympics,
and then, facing the rough lines of yourself, suffer
again the doubtful desire to decipher
the beauty of another evening, the alembic

served hot to your soul, the vacancy
of your thoughts that move like bits of ash
across the sky's magnificent cliché—
suffer this, but note what you can see:

an infinity of disparate bits,
cigarette butts, parked cars, empty bottles,
and people held together somehow, by some dull
weight, or by a flowering vine that buds

invisibly into the heads of billions—
and hear the buzz of traffic, a saxophone,
some voices while somebody considers heaven
and tries to sleep a stone's throw from the lions.

UNUSUAL CLOUD FORMATIONS

Fish bones and bowlers hang over the mountains,
and people below think, "The world's too mundane."
They dream lavish things. "But nothing's so lovely
as your hand," thinks the dog who's troubled by fleas.

Dreams fall like snow on complacent pillows;
loose bones drift down toward the mountains below.
And each sleeping head carves an enormous valley
in the crust of the pillow, where dark hangs heavily.

Today's clouds look like fish bones and bowlers;
if I don't wash my glasses, my life is a blur.
Fierce light parts the curtains and pools on a table,
but I'm not seeing double; I'm not seeing double.

The sun breaks from a cloud and erases our shadows;
the moon breaks from the earth and slides under our toenails.
The wind blows so hard that it opens the windows;
one does wonder what one does wonder one does.

Our hearts can be fashioned in all pretty colors,
but the people who lose them want nothing in particular.
A large oak branches out with green branches;
where its soul wanders is anyone's guess.

A child plays a game; she counts up to ten
and sits with her back to the bowler-topped mountains.
The mountains watch time fly south with a heron,
and before the child looks, they turn, and they run.

A FERRY CROSSING

On the horizon, a floating layer cake:
four white tiers above the sound's blue plate
rippling underneath the ferry's aching
deck, and underneath a kingfisher.
So pretty and tranquil. Without effort,
it seems, she bears tons across the waves; perhaps
her passage hourly back and forth
keeps this bit of sound a polished glass
to let the crossing passengers reflect.
I get in line; my eyes follow the road
that dives off the wharf into the shallows.
My cares, careening with the momentum
my car had gathered speeding for this boat,
plunge off the edge like lemmings. Twenty minutes
'til the next crossing, so cut the engine,
dip the toes in, maybe a train will pass.
Maybe I'll fall asleep, hugging the wheel
like a life ring . . .

Where am I going? To the other side,
a region of hard and glistening shadow,
the unexamined darkness of a seed.
It seems so easy, as if the waxing ferry
hauled the vernal equinox. I like this:
I'll be delivered blooming. The road ends, yet
something's still fertile. So I go to get
coffee from a roadside stand, and sit
behind the wheel again. A gull upends,
reflects a boomerang across the windshield,

flying from the stones of uncaged children.
Creosote exhales from the pilings;
smelling of camphor, it mixes with the fish smell
and the coffee smell: strong, dark,
staining, a recipe for memory.
Cars roll toward the shoreline like the waves.
Come, suburbans, trailers, and coupes:
we haven't parked here just to watch the sunset.
For soon a big ship will pause by the capstan,
and with the day's last rays of light
we all will drain toward her and disappear.

She docks, full, without a sound. Cars file
off like bees into the evening light,
while one by one the engines of three hundred
waiting cars cough to life like dawn birdsongs,
and nothing happens. Does the ferry bask
in her unburdened frame? Perhaps she'd linger
on this empty edge, the waves curling
beneath her, her wandering over, anchored . . .
Why, when joy is to be filled again?
She crosses over, lives for love, moves
only forward while time strums back and forth
across her steely belly (it's time to board.
My tires hum the metal grooves; a man
puts blocks behind my wheels)—and we are thresholds
too—moving, imperceptibly, not jostled
at all, crammed aboard the ferry end to end.
Car doors slam and echo. I head upstairs

to the passenger deck, where the diner
sells soda pop and beer in "Official
Washington State Ferry Reusable
Plastic Cups"—for everything recycles
on the ferry. Ride the USS *Hiatus*
where equipoise comes swaying back and forth
and watch the waves proceed the other way,
swallow some trembling beer and disappear
again, now pressed between mild brines inside
and out, not even once to think about
the pitchy shore, but faultless and afloat
aboard a thousand-ton baptismal font.
A young couple drapes a vinyl sofa,
kissing, careless of the spumy wake
the ferry trails behind her like a veil.
Some children run like pirates in the aisles,
and under the cabin's cold fluorescent beams
a girl's knees and her fashion magazine
reflect onto the sundown's inky window.
Spread across the sound, the pages turn.
Out on deck the air stings, wet and salt.
A single gull flies even with the prow
and seems just to be holding still,
looking sidelong at a young man on deck
smoking, the cigarette's gray curls prowling
a peaked, steel roof. Some dark fish leaps an antic
leap, and the young man stubs out his flame,
teeters, and walks downstairs in the quiet
rising from the silenced engines.

Coasting, it seems, we're meeting land again.
This boat ride ends as soon as it begins.
I'd looked so forward to . . . I can't recall—
but this suspended calm some passengers
found beneath the awnings
overlooking the passing sound, this soft
uncertain ground now meets the dock,
which is oil-stained, pungent, and tangible
as hope (and how like an iceberg hope can knock
you down). The steady ferry pours and pours.

THE HAT OF MISS MAGEE

I saw Miss Magee walking down the road
wearing a hat the size and shape of a Brazil nut.
The clouds hovered, the houses stood,
and Miss Magee looked passionate.

The next day, as she walked the mile to church,
her hat appeared to be a bulging envelope.
The crickets murmured, "cha cha cha,"
and Miss Magee waved, smiling and biting her lip.

On Monday I took a stroll around the block
and saw Miss Magee walking over yonder.
Her hat was indecipherable, a black
shape without boundaries, and wonderful.

And later I went walking. I saw Miss Magee:
how rakishly she wore each passing hour!
Dragonflies and bats veered overhead
and Miss Magee shivered in the evening air.

The following afternoon I took a turn
and spotted Miss Magee: strapped onto her head
was Mr. Bellyache, from Outoftown.
I didn't wave, for she appeared distracted.

And the other day, you'll never guess whom I saw:
Miss Magee. This time up top she wore
nothing but the state of Massachusetts.
It was charming if just a bit small for her.

Early this morning, I walked through the meadow.
The starlings glittered, the chicory bloomed, and I suppose
that more than the world is the hat of Miss Magee
trembling about her wild eyebrows.

WILD

The egret stands still as a glass of milk
by the lagoon, beneath a saw palmetto.
The lagoon shimmers with a school of mackerel,
and then a hand lifts up to close the blinds,
a chorus line of slender bands of metal.
The things we see rarely conform to plans.

Now a paw of sunlight edges through a crack
in the blinds and expands across the wall.
It prowls among the corners, grazes the crackers
on the table, uncurls toward the sofa
where we sit. And once this lucid animal
devours us, it glides off, pacified.

SAN FRANCISCO BAY LANDSCAPE

The calm bay overlaps its grays and greens
while a man-long, blood-red flag ingratiates

itself, billowing into the view. Ample
clouds unfurl. Five doves flap pell-mell

up on ascending pendulums, steel-gray
as the distant bay, startled by

a nosy corgi (the doves are startled,
not the bay), twenty uniformed youngsters

stand on a pier, and seven pelicans
head for Alcatraz Island (laconic

jail birds, a flying chain gang) to disappear
one by one behind a battleship.

Such traffic. Barges, floating low
beneath haphazard stacks of containerized cargo,

trail behind them mere filaments of wake
that grow, as our regrets grow, and make a sailboat rock.

The island attracts the eye, though, the pupil
of the view, the largely floating pupa

anything might crawl from. Surrounded
by the bay, its lush shrubs and red-brown turf

curl like a patch of hair. It would slide seaward
through the Golden Gate, but lost the golden key,

as perhaps the island's one-time denizens
forgot the Golden Rule. Is there any Zen

to captivity? Did any iron cell
ever set its inmate free? Pale celery-

colored shoals lap against the island's skirt.
One sees a little of any landscape.

SONG FOR DANCING

The lilies are tigers. They wave and roar,
and borne on animated shadows, rare

as quiet, evening ripens like a plum.
If I refuse to dance, maybe I'm blooming.

And I should be going. The sun disappears,
with my wallet and keys, into my purse;

the sky spreads its embers, and icy clouds thaw,
and I won't dare to think: I'll just be thought.

A dozen lovers dance by the sea.
Their dreams are smoke; their names are XYZ—

they eat fading roses, and they sing low,
they dance with everyone and dance alone;

the awkward world regains its sense of balance
as they twirl beneath the streamers and balloons,

but when the evening hovers near their heads,
they say "goodnight" and don't forget their hats,

and hear the whole world tick but never tock.
My body's a pond, dear, my mind's a duck,

and once a year it flies away, and once
a year it wants and wants and wants and once

upon a time is written on my heels.
You dance in the valley, and I'll dance on the hills.

MATTER AND RAPTURE

As we sat eating dinner, not talking
but looking at the view, the ship canal
a silver vein beneath the matted clouds,
I seemed to see sublimity annulled
beneath an overbearing complexity.
So much to see, and all of it too close,
the telescope gawked clueless at the city,
and I gawked that way at my water glass,
at how the world swelled outward like a bubble
from its lip. I lifted my spoon: shiny
as the canal, heavy as the globe, full of the pull
of all tangible things that would make me forget
the volatile, half-glimpsed radiance
beyond my reach but within my attention,

and I couldn't say a thing. The sunset
must have been too fine to interrupt;
I sat like stone and watched the sky dissolve
itself—perhaps my apathy was rapture.
Yes, an intimate magnificence
strode in and heaved itself into my face;
so obvious it was invisible,
and so potent it numbed all of my senses—
and all the while I say the world welled from
my water glass, and then it hovered an arm's
reach away. It scorned the oval frame
the glass imposed, it scorned the windows, rooms,
it scorned the two of us eating dinner,
our minds incongruous, our bodies near.

ICEBERG LETTUCE

What vegetable leviathan
extends beneath the dinner table,
an unseen, monstrous green that pulls
the chair out from under our faith

in appearances: see a pale tuft
of leaf on the plate like a wing?
If it flies away, it undoubtedly
will disturb the continental drift

asleep under the salad plate,
the hidden world we forget
as we reach for the smaller fork—
(and now, mouth full, don't speak: politely

chew your leaf of firmament
that's torn and tossed up in vinegar here as
we'll be tossed before its vast
root maybe someday or any moment).

STARGAZING

On certain cloudy evenings I leaf through
my palm-sized Sky Observers' Guide
and skim a dark heaven made clear as day
with color plates and diagrams.
Real stars are never so articulate,
their insubstantial dots hardly connect,
and, unlike these monogrammed planets
in pastels, the night is largely
black and white. Where else can you see
the earth wearing a long necklace
of moons, strung and odd-shaped like freshwater
pearls? Where else do double stars
swing hula hoops, do thirteen suns eclipse
at once like sooty buttercups
and never fade, where else do asteroids
hold still but here, flat on my palm?
When nights are clear I scan the stars and forget
the names and dance steps I have read.
Their brilliance is too far above my head.
But home, thumbing through the guide, sometimes
my thumb inadvertently covers the sun.

Shaded by a crab apple, the little
headstones look like the backs of chairs that sank
into the lawn by the clapboard sanctum,
Congregational, its steeple the delight
of gulls. The headstones are askew, in waving
rows, and each wizened slate like lizard
skin is dappled with spreading, carnation-
like blooms of green lichen, or more like sugar
sprinkled on the stones—and warps absorb
the thoughts: the crowns, rarely rectangular,
are cloverleaf, eared with curlicues,
thin slices of rock rounded by some
stonecutter's art to ape the mild bosoms
of our first and final mothers, irregular

as sympathy is. This is a jaunty
graveyard. I'd like to pause here for three hundred
years, singing gently like a cricket
while my bones collapse, in equipoise
with time and eternity, and visited
by strangers (on tiptoe, curious, civil)
who meander among the brown, shrunken
headstones, astounded—three hundred years! and breathe
life into the names, *Prudence, Pardon,*
Harmony, and consider the burden
history bears, or time's even temper,
gratitude, the soul's arcane ballistics,
and note the posthumously erected,
moss-covered, seven-foot obelisk

for Elisabeth Pabodie, *The first*
white woman born (in 1623)
in New England (down the road you'll see
a monument to the Rhode Island Red,
also bred here; that monument's smaller
but shows a picture of the hen), or read
In memory of Margaret, who should
have been the wife of Mr. Simeon
Palmer, dead in her 64th year. (Your shadow
stretches out on the grass beside her,
folds over some stones.) She's buried adjacent
to Lydia, Mr. Palmer's late wife.
Death's editing is rigorous with life,
distilling it to a few chastening

dates: where are the ordinary days our
memories so carefully inter?
A mind frames its infinite universe
in limited time, and there each universe
slips away, ta-ta, a vanishing point's
black sun we're drawn to and endlessly enter.
Gone before, Called back, a pithy treatise
on virtue—many stones are illegible,
though, or nearly, the chiseled letters leached
away by centuries and salt. Industry
and alphabets will crumble, and so will a stone,
but these stones are kin to the Rock of Ages, and their resonant
gestures ripple across the ground of our reason
(which certain individuals, stunned

or distracted, lose track of—) oh, for
the love of peace, breathe the immortality
here. Yellow hawkweed blooms a litany
of suns, and these gravestones make overtures
to the imagination, are lithic
bookmarks in life's pages. Unperturbable
pilgrims who persevered through bitter, humble
lives, their stones are tanned, smiling, thickly
planted: shoulder to shoulder, some resting
their heads on another's knees, sometimes
two tucked in the same grave, and whole families
together—dear, it's flesh that guarantees
our solitude, not death. No need to pity
such community—nudging a bit

too close, in fact, for that fellow riding
the lawn mower to fit between the rows,
so the grass grows long between the stones,
and the yellow hawkweeds don't lose their heads
as if with sorrow—o soar, you buried
souls, rejoice! You do defy the reaper,
reaching up so verdantly. I wonder,
are the graves in modern cemeteries
placed to accommodate the diameters
of lawn mowing tractors? *Whir* . . . one turn
deserves another, and the fellow's going
away, as we all will, someday, to some
unusual place whose sumptuous
description's effaced in the going.

VANISHING POINTS

The dead man's float, caught in eddies:
a wasp in my kitchen circles dazedly

from window to window, its low buzz
rattling the pans. It climbs the lapis

panes now, near the lace curtain. Sweet cousin,
amble on along that frozen sky . . .

trapped it. It's safe, beneath a glass tumbler—
but glaring with magnified ire, a blurry

pupil in a highball eyeball—oh, wild
Cyclops, now your venomous stare turns gold

and black toward me. And what can I do but hold
this cataract distractedly bottled:

"Frozen Niagara in Mammoth Cave,"
a postcard from Kentucky, yesterday:

an enormous lip of rock and crystalline
stalactites descending—"we still

pray for you—" a long arm's length away.
I reach it, ease it between the wasp and the window pane,

press it tight, right the glass. The wasp
steps upside down on the postcard's lustrous

image, long legs tickle my paper fingers,
as the wasp waits, its sickle abdomen curving

down (prudent stricture, paradoxically,
can calico a life with bits of rapture)—

I step outdoors and roll back the frozen
stone of Kentucky from the new risen.

ACKNOWLEDGMENTS

Grateful acknowledgement is made to these journals, in which the following poems (some in earlier versions) appeared: *Antioch Review* ("Vanishing Points," "What a Bird Said"); *Boston Review* ("Blues and Reds," "The Hat of Miss Magee," "San Francisco Bay Landscape," "Song for Dancing," "Unusual Cloud Formations"); *Carolina Quarterly* ("Stargazing"); *The Fiddlehead* ("The Cemetery on the Commons," "View from the Bluff," "Zeros, Veers,"); *Fine Madness* ("Matter and Rapture," "Walking"); *Paris Review* ("The Beam," "Self-Portrait, Double Exposed," "Waiting"); *Poetry* ("Ants," "Iceberg Lettuce," "Wild"); *Poetry Northwest* ("The Cleaning"); *Southwest Review* ("The Zoo," "View from the Porch"); *Third Coast* ("Falling Backward"); *Western Humanities Review* ("Arvida Community," "Geese and Billie Holiday," "The Oracle"); *Yale Review* ("Seattle to Boston," "Electric Storm on Brayton Point," "Lunch by the Construction Site and After").

This manuscript was completed with the help of a Wallace Stegner Fellowship at Stanford University, and many thanks to the generosity of that program. Many thanks also to the Creative Writing Program at the University of Washington, to the King County Arts Commission, Seattle, Washington, for a Special Projects Grant, and to Centrum Center for the Arts.

Joanie Mackowski's poems have been widely published in such journals as the *Antioch Review,* the *Boston Review, Poetry,* the *Yale Review,* and the *Paris Review.* Currently a Creative Writing Fellow at the University of Missouri–Columbia, she is the recipient of numerous prizes including the 2000 Rona Jaffe Foundation Writer's Award and a Wallace Stegner Fellowship from Stanford University for 1998–2000. Mackowski earned a B.A. from Wesleyan University, as well as an M.F.A. and an M.A. from the University of Washington. *The Zoo* was selected for the 2000 Associated Writing Programs' Award in Poetry by Li-Young Lee.